I KNOW WHO I AM

ON THE FAMILY TREE

A Children's Guide to Genealogy

Written by Denise I. Griggs

I KNOW WHO I AM
ON THE FAMILY TREE

A Children's Guide to Genealogy

Denise I. Griggs © 2024
ISBN 979-8-9867644-4-3

Library of Congress Control Number: 2024901570

Published by:
Glass Tree Books
P.O. Box 278475
Sacramento, CA 95827-8475

Andrew Yong, Book Illustrator
Jenneth Dyck, Cover Design

Dedicated to my parents and our ancestors from:

The Continents of:

Africa

Asia

Europe

AND

The United States of America:

Arkansas

Kentucky

Louisiana

Maryland

Mississippi

Missouri

Tennessee

Virginia

INTRODUCTION

As you research your family history and genealogy, you will link your family history to many of your school subjects, such as:

Geography
Government
Social Studies
World history

With this knowledge, you can compare the life events of your ancestors to many world events. Do you know how? Things happened to them, around them, and yet, your family affected the world! You might discover relatives from another country or continent. Too, your ancestors might have been from a combination of continents and other nationalities. No matter their background, you will find impressive discoveries about your family.

Some families had ancestors enlisted as soldiers in major wars like the American Revolution, the Civil War, World Wars I and II, the Korean War, and the Vietnam War. Over the years, discussing these stories so much, sometimes the facts get all mixed up. Sometimes they might not be true. The goal is to get to the truth of your lineage so you can help share the information with your parents, and later to your children and future generations.

We all learn from the successes and failures in the lives of our family. Even if their story is good or not so good, we should always remember our ancestors. So, it's up to all of us to tell the story accurately.

WHAT ARE YOUR INTERESTS?

Do you have the following talents or skills? Are there interests you could add to this list?

ART	ADMINISTRATION
BIOLOGY	ANALYSIS
COOKING	CURIOSITY
HISTORY	DETERMINATION
MATH	DREAMER
SCIENCE	FAITH
SEWING	PLANNER
SPORTS	TEAM PLAYER
TEACHING	INQUISITIVE

By using your interests and skills, you can use them to your advantage while learning about your family's history and genealogy. Learning and understanding your family's history can help improve your hobbies, skills, school, and life.

Genealogy and research are some of the many activities you will enjoy. For some, it will become a favorite hobby, or a lifetime adventure for others!

FUN ACTIVITIES FROM YOUR ANSWERS

Working together, everyone becomes a type of <u>genealogy detective</u> or forensic investigator. It will take you on an adventure to discover and solve clues and events.

Use YOUR creativity like the ones below:

1. Make Sheriff badges for the little children with their name on them.

2. Give notebooks to the Inquisitive ones who like to ask questions.

3. The Analyst helps to interpret information and dates. Is it true or incorrect?

4. The Administrator is the record keeper for the genealogy binder and creates a timeline.

5. The Artist draws charts and potential pictures from descriptions of ancestors and decorates them as needed.

6. The ones who love science and biology work together on the DNA project and information.

7. Create your own detective's name, like Detective Truth, Detective Gotcha, Forensic Mastermind.

PREPARATION

Before anyone begins their family history, politely ask your parents, grandparents, or other relatives to help. If they do not have the time for so many questions, just be patient. They might help you at a more convenient time.

If they do not want to discuss it, nor enjoy their history or genealogy as much as you would like, it is o.k. They will still be proud of your research and discoveries as you work on your family history. Who knows? They might want YOU to present it at your next family reunion!

Sometimes at family gatherings, your grandparents, uncles, aunts, and cousins have the answers you need. There will always be surprises to discover along the way!

As you begin the investigation of your family history, never throw away a document, a note, or a family story, because all of them are CLUES! Family genealogy detectives will need to compare and share the information when the family gets together to discuss it.

Let the Adventure Begin!

WHERE DO I BEGIN?

? ? ?

To begin your genealogy research, you must first decide upon a goal.

<u>Goal</u>: An aim, a purpose.

Your goal is to uncover your family history. This is your general goal or the big picture. Your next goal will be more specific.

<u>Specific Goal</u>: Definite, exact, on purpose.

A specific goal is the action necessary to accomplish your goal. First, you must decide:

1. What do I want to find out?
2. Who has the information I need?
3. When did it occur?
4. Where do I look for other information?
5. How do I put the information in order?
6. How do I plan?

<u>Plan</u>: A method for accomplishing something.

Having a plan helps you stay focused on your overall goal and make the steps necessary to discover answers. It might seem like an enormous task, but all successful research begins with a plan.

Once you begin the first and simplest steps towards your goal, you can then begin to take the larger steps toward learning more about your family history.

1. Write down what you know.

2. Wherever you have a blank, don't give up! It's merely a CLUE to solve.

3. Decide who in your family might be able to answer the question. If no one can, it becomes a research adventure.

4. Begin your chart of ancestors and discover how far back in time you can locate them.

You will discover ancestors for many generations. Some people have researched back to their 32nd generation! By the time anyone gets to this point, they have used many genealogy resources and professional genealogists. However, they had to start at the beginning too!

To begin, use the ancestor chart on the next page, make copies of it, make your own chart, or use one from the Internet. Begin with yourself and your parents. Do not worry if you do not have all the names and dates just yet, they are simply CLUES.

Notes and Clues:

FAMILY HISTORY

_____

(Your name - Include Your Nickname)

Mom's Name: _____

(Include everyone's Nickname)   *(Always use a woman's <u>maiden</u>/birth name)*

Mom's Father: _____

Mom's Mother: * _____

Mom's Grandfather: _____

Mom's Grandmother: * _____

Dad's Name: _____

Dad's Father: _____

Dad's Mother: * _____

Dad's Grandfather: _____

Dad's Grandmother: * _____

Were you able to get the names of three generations of your ancestors? If so, wonderful! If not, these blank spaces are clues too!

Your next <u>specific</u> <u>goal</u> will be to discover a way to get the rest of the information. Will you need to call your relatives to help you? Just remember: if they do not wish to talk about it right now, it is o.k., give them more time. You can always get answers and information later or from another family member.

<u>Notes and Clues</u>:

THE BEGINNING

The best way to learn about your family history is to begin asking questions. You must go to the best person you know. Do you know who this person is?

Hint: The answer is in the mirror!

Begin with YOURSELF!! Yes, "lovely you!"

The best way to ensure everyone knows something about you is for YOU to write it yourself. It's called an autobiography.

Autobiography: When a person writes the story of their own life.

Who are YOU?

- Who do you look like?
- When were you born?
- Who are your parents?
- Do you have siblings?
- Who are your friends?
- What do you like to do for fun?
- What are your hobbies?
- Do you have a pet?
- What is your favorite color?
- What is your favorite food?

On a separate sheet of paper, write your answers to these questions.

You may not know all things about yourself, like your first words, or when your first tooth appeared, but write down what you do know. The rest of the answers about yourself will be one of your specific goals. You will have to ask your parents or another relative for the answers.

Do you realize your family history will never be complete? Why? Because with each new birth, you and the members of your family will continue to add future generations to it!

<u>Generation</u>: Your family from one ancestor to the next.
(You-your Father/Mother-your Grandparents-your Great Grandparents)

Imagine! Over one hundred years from now, someone in your family will want to know all about you!

<u>Notes and Clues</u>:

MY AUTOBIOGRAPHY
(Some events will always be different from your siblings and cousins)

Written by: _____   Today's Date: _____
               Your Name

Birth Date/Where born: _____

Time you were born: _____

Weight/Length: lbs. _____ ounces _____ inches _____

Eye Color: _____

Hair Color: _____

Your Father: _____

Your Mother: _____

Your Sisters: _____

Your Brothers: _____

Your Pet(s): _____

Favorite Color(s): _____

Favorite Sport(s): _____

Favorite Book(s): _____

Best Friend(s): _____

Your Hobbies: _____

Favorite Music: _____

Favorite Foods: _____

WHY SHOULD I KNOW MY GENEALOGY?

The questions people often ask are, "Why should I know my genealogy or family history, and why is it so important to know?"

It is extremely important! As you begin to study your family, you will uncover facts about how your ancestors fit into world events, local history, social studies, geography, and politics. Not only will you learn about where they lived, but you will also learn about the people who impacted their lives, good or not-so-good.

Although your family began in one country, town, and state, they could have moved from another country, or from town to town, or state to state. Why and when did they move? Where did they move to? Sometimes families leave their hometowns in groups for safety, assistance, purpose, and confidence. Some families stayed in the same area for generations.

Safety: A long time ago, it was safer for families to live together, or next door to one another. Often, if others knew somcone had a large family, they would not cause trouble with them because they knew the entire family would get involved.

Assistance: At one time, families had to chop down trees to build their homes. For their food, they plowed their land, raised crops, and planted gardens around their homes. They also stored their food for use throughout the year. Some of it they sold or exchanged to obtain other needed supplies. Most families also made their own clothes and blankets. Whenever one family needed extra help, all the families worked together to get it done.

Purpose: Some families were skilled craftsmen such as carpenters, blacksmiths, weavers, and seamstresses. Families taught their skills to their children and grandchildren to ensure their future generations could earn money to survive.

Confidence: Knowing about your ancestors gives you confidence. It helps you determine how you want to live, or not live your life. It is better to know the good AND the not-so-good things about your family, rather than have someone else tell you.

Now you are ready to add to your knowledge!

Notes and Clues:

GENEALOGY DETECTIVES LOOK BACK IN TIME

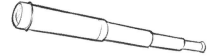

<u>Genealogy</u>: A line of descent from one ancestor to another.

Genealogy research is not to gather information to use as a weapon against anyone. It is meant to add to your knowledge of yourself and the choices your family made in life. This knowledge of your ancestors gives you confidence! Remember: your ancestors made decisions and had to live with the consequences of their choices, just like we all do.

<u>Evidence</u>: Proof; Facts of Events.

When researching your family's genealogy, you must be a good investigator, like a detective, who looks for solid, unshakeable evidence and facts.

<u>Facts</u>: The truth about events.

Facts or proof help solve unknown answers. Determine the best way to proceed, and then ask questions of others to help find the answers you need.

As you gather clues to prove or disprove the mysteries in your family's history, you are the Detective who will solve these mysteries. With time, you will become an "Ace Genealogist!"

NECESSARY SUPPLIES

For your investigation, you will need the following items:

(Always have money just in case you need to make copies or buy something needed)

Address Book	Computer	Notepads	Storage bin(s)
Binder – 8x10	Dictionary	Pencils/Pens	Tape Recorder
Camera	Highlighter pens	Plain Paper	USB drives
Card Holder	Internet access	Portable Scanner	**Genealogy
Cards - 3x5 or 5x7	Local & World Maps	Printer	Software Access
Cell phone	Magnifying Glass	Sheet Protectors	*Misc costs

· <u>Address Book</u>: When at family reunions or visiting relatives, let them know what you are doing. Ask if you can add their names, addresses, phone number(s), and emails to your "genealogy" address book. Next to their name, note how you are related. Always be courteous when you call or write. If you receive a letter or email with family information from a relative or friend, place it in your binder. Call to thank them or send a Thank-You card.

· <u>Camera/Cell Phone</u>: Take pictures when you visit relatives or at family reunions. When visiting their homes, politely ask if you can take a picture of their ancestor's pictures. If you bring your portable scanner, ask if you can scan their pictures. Be sure to print the name(s) of the person in the picture.

· <u>Cards - 3x5 or 5x7</u>: Use cards to notate where you found family information on the Internet and in books. This is called a source.

- <u>Dictionary</u>: If you do not understand a name or word, always look it up. Never guess!

- <u>Map/Magnifying Glass</u>: Use a magnifying glass to look at maps of where your relatives lived, so you can retrace their movements.

- <u>Notepad/Pencils/Recording Device</u>: Write down what others tell you, even if it does not sound right, it is a clue. Or, with their permission, use your tape recorder or cell phone to record their statements and recollections. Reread or listen to it later, as there will be clues you might have missed while they were answering your questions.

- <u>Sheet Protectors/Binder</u>: Sheet protectors keep pictures and copies of your documents free from damage while in your binder. When attending family reunions, take only copies of what is in your binder, just in case it gets lost.

- With a library card, many city libraries have computers available to use free of charge to search genealogy software. In many cities, "FamilySearch" Centers also offer free use of their genealogy software, copiers, and books. Also, for a small fee, they will order microfilm and microfiche records from the city and county you're researching. Some libraries and centers have classes about genealogy research.

  Genealogy Detectives - prepare for your first clue!

CLUE #1

WHAT'S IN A NAME?

Do you know the meaning of your first, middle, and last names? Do you know its origin, or where it began? The meaning of your name is an important clue to where your ancestors came from, or what your parents were thinking when they named you. Your name might remind them of the love they had for each other when you were born, or it describes a character they desire to see in you after you become an adult. Sometimes babies are named after a favorite ancestor, parent, or best friend.

Meaning of Your Names

(You might need a book of names or the Internet to answer these questions)

_____	_____	_____
First	**Middle**	**Last**

In What Countries Did Your Names Originate?

_____	_____	_____

<u>**Notes and Clues:**</u>

CLUE #2

IT'S ONLY A VOWEL - A, E, I, O, U

Sometimes, when researching genealogy, you will discover different spellings of your last name. Using my name as an example, these are the numerous spellings I found for my name.

Example: Griggs = Graigs, Greggs, Griggis, Craig

What vowels can you use to misspell your name?

_____   _____   _____

Sometimes, people change their names for several reasons. It makes it easier to shorten their names for clarity or to make it easier to pronounce or understand. Immigrants who came from other countries might have had a name like Westovich. They might have changed it to Westover or West, or a name like Abramovich to Abram.

Over 165 years ago, there were slaves in America. Once freed, they changed their names from their enslaver's name back to their parent's name or they created a new name for themselves. For instance, a slave might have been named Joe Brown while working on the Brown Plantation. After freedom (Emancipation), Joe Brown might have changed his name to Joe Freeman because he was now a free man. Again, the name might have changed to the name Fremont.

CLUE #3

FAMILY STORIES

Family stories are often repeated from one generation to the next. Sometimes, no one remembers how the story began. One thing about stories, even if you do not have the proof, these stories will always have clues to point you to where you can find the proof!

What stories have you heard about your family's history and background? Ask other family members what they know about the stories. Do not be surprised if you hear 2-3 versions of the same story because everyone's memory is not the same. Parents, siblings, and different age groups have different perspectives of the same story. Even twins differ in their views or memory of the same story!

No one is wrong or fibbing. It's just that everyone has a different view, perspective, or memory, but everyone's version has many clues. Keep them all written in your notepad or on note cards. One day, you will find one or two things to be true, while other things are incorrect. Knowing both the correct and incorrect parts will be extremely helpful in getting to the facts.

On the following page, write down the viewpoints of three people regarding the same story. If you need additional paper, make copies of the page, or use a separate sheet of paper, and place it in your genealogy binder.

Story 1:

_____

_____

_____

Story 2:

_____

_____

_____

Story 3:

_____

_____

_____

What are the similarities? What are the differences?

<u>Notes and Clues</u>:

CLUE #4

CENSUS RECORDS

In the United States, there are Population Census Schedules to search for records of your family's history. They began in 1790 and were recorded every ten years. These records are released to the public 72 years after they are recorded. An example is the 1950 census. It was not released to the public until 2022.

Early census records named only the men in the house and used tally marks for the number and age of the women and children. Later census records named everyone living in the house. Some of these records stated how they were related and those who were boarders or workers. Some records stated whether the home was rented or owned, what their jobs were, if they owned any land or property, and the estimated value of it. Most census records during the 18th and 19th centuries in the United States counted the number of slaves living on the property. Most slaves were not listed by name but were listed by gender, complexion, and age.

When checking the census records for clues, there are columns across the top of the page. Some census records reflect who is the head of the house, if they're married, how long they have been married, and how old they were when they first married. Some state how many births the woman had, how many children were still living, approximately when they were born, and their current ages. It also reflected whether they could read or write, their race, the state where they were born, and if they knew, where their parents were born.

As with any document, mistakes can be made. Examples of mistakes were about someone's age and birth year. Many times, the ages did not match up every census year because people did not know the exact day or year they were born.

Sometimes a person was misidentified as a female rather than a male, or vice versa. Some census recorders spelled names as they heard them, but not the way they should have been spelled. An example is the name Phyllis. Sometimes it was spelled as Fillis, Fylis, Phillis, or Felice.

<u>Notes and Clues:</u>

CLUE #5

CENSUS RECORDS

Unfortunately, many people identified themselves by their nicknames because they didn't know they had a birth name. When a census worker couldn't find someone at home, the neighbors would give him their nicknames too because they were unaware of their real names.

NICKNAME EXAMPLE

Tom and his siblings were orphaned at an early age, but remembered the names of their parents, Bud, and Sadie. While researching records in the state and county where Tom was born, his mother's first name was recorded differently when she was a child. The 1910 census records state her birth name was Sarah. Sadie was her nickname! Still, records of Tom's father, Bud, could not be found.

Upon researching the 1920 census, Tom's parents were married, but their last name (surname) was misspelled! Their last name had an additional "i" added between the g and s, so it was spelled as "Griggis." How did Tom know they were his family? He recognized their nicknames! The children listed were Tom's siblings.

Another discovery was Tom's father's birth name. It was Luther. Bud was Luther's nickname! Tom nor his siblings knew the birth names of their parents until they saw this record.

1920 U.S. CENSUS *(partial)*

NAME	RELATION	
OF EACH PERSON WHOSE PLACE OF ABODE ON JANUARY 1, 1920, WAS IN THIS FAMILY	RELATIONSHIP TO HEAD OF HOUSEHOLD	
Griggis, Luther	Head	*Nickname "Bud"*
" Sadie	Wife	*Actual Name "Sarah"*
" Dessie	Daughter	*Actual Name "Odessa"*
" Rosa L.	Daughter	*Actual Name "Rosalie"*
" Ellmer	Son	*Nickname "Pete"**
" Christiner	Daughter	*Actual Name "Christine"*
" Anna	Daughter	*Actual Name "Savanna"*

Tom also remembered his paternal grandfather's odd first name but was not sure how to spell it. By using vowels to check unusual ways of sounding out his first and last names, Tom found his grandfather on the 1880 census, living at home with his parents and younger brothers. Tom discovered the names of his great grandparents and their nine sons! Further, on several census records, the first name of Tom's grandfather was spelled five unusual ways, and he was listed as three different races! It was proven by the names of his family members living with him.

CLUE #6

SOUNDS LIKE IT SOUNDS

To better search for a name from the main census, a Soundex Coding Guide was created for the years 1880-1930. It reflects where family names are on the actual census page in a state and county. This code reduces anyone's last name to one letter and three numbers. An example is the number for the last name Ross. It is R-200.

Soundex numbers for each family depended upon how census takers spelled their names. Sometimes various dialects pronounced it differently, like someone in the South does not sound like someone from the North. One example is the name Brown. Depending on a person's dialect, it could have been written as Brawn, Brow, Browne, or Braan. Some people could not read or write, so they didn't know how to spell or verify the spelling of their first or last names.

Write an example of unusual ways to spell your name.

_____   _____   _____

You may also search the Internet for the Soundex Coding Guide to get the code to your last name. Then follow the instructions to see how it was done.

To test your skills at finding the code to your last name, use the Soundex Coding Guide. Print your last name here:

_____

LETTERS	CODE
B,P,F,V	1
C,S,G,J,K,Q,X,Z	2
D,T	3
L	4
M,N	5
R	6

Use the above Soundex Code then follow the example below to find the code for your last name.

Example: MY NAME: Griggs

1. Write the first initial of your last name. ___G___ Put a dash (-) after the first initial, ex. G -.

2. Cross out all the vowels A, E, I, O, and U. Then, if you have the letters W, H, and Y in your last name, cross them out too. Example (cross out the vowel "i") = G-RGGS

3. If your last name has two of the same letters together, like the two "gg's" in the name Griggs, cross out one "g" = G-RGS

4. If the final letter is on the same code line as another, Ex. S is on the same line as G , cross it out = G-RG.

5. Now there are 2 letters remaining after the dash
   Ex. <u>G-RG.</u>

6. Next, add a zero to make it three numbers. Ex. = <u>G-620</u>.

**You must add a zero, or two, to make a total of three numbers. If the name is misspelled, it will be different, like Griggis is G-622.

What is the code for your last name?

_____ - _____

(letter – numbers)

Notes and Clues:

CLUE #7

FAMILY DOCUMENTS

You can find valuable information and clues about your family on birth, marriage, and death certificates. If you do not have copies, you can order them from the state where they were born, married, or died. If any information is missing, it is another clue.

BIRTH CERTIFICATE

Birth name: _____

Date of birth: _____

Father's Name/Age: _____

Father's Occupation: _____

Mother's Name/Age: _____

Mother's Occupation: _____

Doctor/Hospital: _____

Midwife Name: _____

When birth recorded: _____

City/County/State: _____

Relationship to You: _____

MARRIAGE CERTIFICATE

Groom's Name/Age: _____

Bride's Name/Age: _____

Date of Application: _____

Date of Marriage: _____

Pastor/Judge Name: _____

Witnesses: _____

Date Filed: _____

Relationship to You: _____

DEATH CERTIFICATE

Who Died: _____

(Their full name and Nickname)

Date of Death: _____

His/her Birth Date: _____

City of Birth: _____

His/Her Father: _____

His/Her Mother: _____

His/Her Spouse(s) _____

Informant: _____

Funeral Home: _____

CLUE #8

OBITUARY

An obituary is written after someone dies. The family pays to have it printed in the newspaper or given out at the funeral. In it are the details of the person's life. Sometimes pictures are included. The information comes from the family or public records. What can you discover in an obituary? Get one from your parents, or the newspaper and complete this chart.

Name of Deceased: _____

(Their full name and Nickname)

Spouse(s): _____

Names of Children: _____

Grandchildren: _____

Brothers/Sisters: _____

Occupation: _____

Nieces/Nephews: _____

Best/Special Friend(s): _____

Where Funeral Held: _____

Doctor(s), Hospital: _____

Cemetery Name: _____

Date of Burial: _____

This format is good to use when writing an obituary for anyone. Sometimes obituaries have conflicting information because no one had all the correct facts when it was written. Corrections to an obituary can be made and attached to the original one in the family binder.

Often, families set aside a day to clean their family burial plots and headstones. While there, one of the ways to recover a faded name from a headstone or tombstone is to tape plain paper on it and gently rub over it with a dark crayon, or charcoal. The name and dates will appear from the faded indentations. The cemetery office on site also might have the information you need.

Now that you now know how to write an obituary correctly, be sure to let your family know how it is done. Choose a place to keep all obituaries, like in a drawer or plastic bin. After years of collecting them, you can donate them to a local library whose staff might digitize them for the history of the person and community in which they lived.

<u>Notes and Clues</u>:

CLUE #9

FAMILY REUNIONS

Families gather at reunions to reunite and renew their unity and legacy. They celebrate their ancestors who sacrificed for them to have better lives! Everyone shares news, pictures, and memories. It's also a time to dedicate, honor, and remember those who have passed away between reunions.

Event nights include a Meet and Greet Social, attending an awards banquet, and fashion show. Entertainment can be listening to a guest speaker, or a family-friendly comedian. Talent shows and singing contests are always a welcome addition. The host describes the accomplishments of the family, from the oldest known ancestor to all descendants!

An exciting event is Picnic day! Fun activities are planned for everyone. All ages take part in the 3-legged race, egg toss, water balloon fights, or board and card games. Children love races, and teens enjoy sports like baseball, volleyball, and basketball. Some food events are bobbing for apples, pie or watermelon eating contests, and Best Cook Awards.

To end the picnic, the host plans a funny activity for a few adults to take part in. Ours is the "Fried Chicken-Neck Eating" contest! It is hilarious to watch! Yikes! Whatever you do - don't swallow! The grand prize is all the empty soda cans and water bottles from our reunion area.

What funny activity does your family celebrate at reunions?

_____

HELPFUL SUGGESTIONS

You and your cousins can be an immense help to your family by giving them ideas for children's activities.

What Was The Most Fun?

What Games Did You Play?

Where Was It Held?

Where Do You Want To Have It Next? *(city, state, or Country)*

Who Did You Meet For The First Time?

Who Should You Invite Next Time?

CLUE # 10

FAVORITE FOODS

The foods your family cooks or likes better than others are important clues. The food might be a hint of where your ancestors lived in another country, nation, or the world. Many of these foods are brought to family reunions, or only cooked on special holidays.

There are family cooks who never tell the ingredients in their best food dishes. They keep the ingredients to themselves, or only with their children, keeping it a family secret! Sometimes families share their favorite recipes with one another and put them into a family cookbook as a fundraiser for the next reunion.

In the past, some families only had a little flour or cornmeal, water, and a vegetable or two to cook but it was still delicious! Have you ever heard of Tomato Cobbler, Vinegar Pie, or Waterless Cake? Delicious!

Sometimes, parents would make up special names for meals so their children would want to eat it. Some meals were called, "this is going to be the best meal you will ever eat" or "Daddy's Garbage Breakfast." Somehow having a funny name for the food seems to make it taste much better!

Notes and Clues:

Fill in the blanks about your favorite foods.

Best Meal(s): _____

Best Dessert(s): _____

The Best Cook In Your Family: _____

Your Family's Famous, Favorite, Or Secret Recipe?
(This might be a trick question)

_____

_____

_____

_____

Notes and Clues:

CLUE #11

WHAT IS YOUR FAVORITE FOOD(S)?

FROM WHAT COUNTRY, DID THESE FOODS ORIGINATE?

(Do not guess. Use a dictionary or the Internet. You might be surprised)

Pancakes

Ice Cream

Taco

Pizza

Pineapple

Coconut

CLUE #12

WHAT IS YOUR ALL-TIME FAVORITE SPORT(S)?

IN WHICH COUNTRY DID THESE SPORTS ORIGINATE?

(Do not guess. Use a dictionary or the Internet. You might be surprised)

Basketball

Soccer

Football

Baseball

Tennis

Golf

Ice Skates

Skis

CLUE #13

WHAT DO YOU WANT TO BE WHEN YOU GROW UP?

Your goals in life, and what you want to become when you grow up, are also important clues. Do you have a natural ability like singing or drawing? Do you want a job like one of your parents, family members, or someone famous? Why did you choose this profession? Did it come from your ancestors? Will you teach this skill or profession to your children and grandchildren?

Nothing is impossible to achieve if you are determined to work for it. After you decide what you want to do with your life, you will have to set goals for your future and complete them. It might require high school, college, or a trade school education. After working for a while, you might need to take courses to improve your skills. Certainly, you must do well on your job and more so if it's a company you created.

First, you must believe you can do it! Next, get the best information available about your profession, even if you decide to be a homemaker and raise children. Secondly, carefully choose your friends and associates who will help you stay on the right path. At all times, make sure you don't involve yourself with people who might derail your life. Be a leader and not a follower!

Your future depends on what YOU make happen. Be sure to seek good advice from those who know how to help accomplish your goals. They can be school counselors, parents, and people you read about who share their lives, failures, and successes. It is never too late to start all over again if you do not give up on yourself!

No one can stop you from accomplishing your dreams and goals, except you, lovely you! You must be determined to stay focused and on the right path, even if no one else is on the path with you. You should finish anything you begin.

What do you want your descendants to know about you in the future? Most records are public knowledge and can be accessed by anyone. Therefore, make yourself, your family, and your descendants proud!

Use the space below to write about what you want to become in life and how you might accomplish it. Use additional paper if needed.

_____

_____

_____

_____

_____

_____

_____

CLUE #14

WHERE IN THE WORLD?

PANGAEA

A SUPER CONTINENT

Did you know there used to be only one continent in the world? It was called Pangaea, a supercontinent. It looked like the picture above. An artist might visualize it as a man flexing his muscles, a scientist might visualize it as an embryo or amoeba, and another might see it as the capital letter C. Still, it is a clue!

When Pangaea began to drift apart into separate continents, the land bridges to various continents broke away. This is why artifacts of various cultures and animal bones are found on different continents all over the world!

As the land separated, it eventually formed the seven major continents in the world today. Those continents are Africa, Antarctica, Asia, Australia, Europe, North America, and South America. To prove it, buy an inexpensive world map, cut out all the continents and islands. Then, like puzzle pieces, connect them together. They will look like the continent Pangaea!

Over time, our ancestors traveled across landmasses, oceans, and seas to hunt and interact with other people. In doing so, our ancestors might be a combination of several nationalities! Everyone has family members who come from one or more of these continents. This is an interesting fact and another clue!

What continent did your original ancestors come from? Were they from a large continent, or a small island? Were they fair or dark skin? What nationality were they? It does not matter where they came from, and no one must be ashamed of any part of their heritage! Why? Because the ancestors of most families are from cultures, ethnicities, and nationalities from other parts of the world.

Name the continent(s) from which your family came?

_____

- The year they migrated to this country. _____

- Other states they lived in? _____

- Other cities they lived in? _____

- Other counties they lived in? _____

CLUE #15

DNA

DNA is the newest form to estimate where your ancestors came from with just a saliva sample. SPIT!! Most DNA kits use saliva to determine the ethnic percentages of your ancestors up to three to five generations back in time!

Some people have a combination of ethnicities. Many people are often surprised to find out they are not 100% of any ethnicity, no matter what they look like.

Siblings inherit 50% of their DNA genes from each parent, but the DNA mixtures are unique to each one. Siblings will look similar, but not the same. Parents' genes determine such things as their child's hair and eye color as well as skin tone, along with many other traits. Identical twins start with the same genes, but before birth, slight differences occur.

Y-DNA refers to the DNA found on the Y chromosome in males and is only passed from father to son. However, both males and females inherit their mother's mtDNA.

NOTES AND CLUES:

A DNA EXCEPTION

Identical twins should take two different DNA tests to ensure the accuracy of their ethnic percentages. Look at the following example.

DNA Company 1 (twin 1)

Africa	Europe	Asia
58.6%	39.9%	1.5%

DNA Company 2 (twin 2)

Africa	Europe	So. America
60%	39%	1.0%

From the twin's results, look at a map or timeline to see how these countries might have interacted or coexisted with one another.

Obtain permission to ask the oldest family member to take a DNA test because their ethnicity percentages go further back than yours. Then, add their information to your family binder.

After getting all DNA results, the real fun begins! Dig out your history books, maps, timelines, and what you know about different explorers. You will discover how nations crossed paths to potentially become your ancestors.

What are the historical possibilities or major events that happened to cause your ancestors to move from one continent to another? Was it famine, slavery, persecution, or hope?

<u>**Notes and Clues:**</u>

CLUE #16

TIPS TO TRACE YOUR FAMILY ORIGINS

Here are some helpful research tips to assist you with tracing your family origins:

- Families and groups left their countries because of wars, and some records might no longer exist.

- Various European immigrants came through Ellis Island in New York, from 1892-1954.

- Many Africans were enslaved in various countries through the slave routes from Africa to the Caribbean, South America, and North America. This route was known as the Middle Passage of the Triangular Trade System.

- Some slaves of various nationalities fled to Canada and Mexico.

- People, past and present, of all nationalities and ethnicities, have lived, worked, intermarried, and had other relationships with one another.

- People existed in countries before explorers came to their shores. One example is the native Indian tribes living in North America before the Europeans arrived.

- Some countries have excellent church baptismal records dating back hundreds of years, such as the Catholic dioceses.

- Often people traveled by different routes in America such as the Natchez Trace, the Oregon Trail, the Trail of Tears, and the Three Chopped Way. There are trails and routes that no longer exist, but you can still find them online, or in county history books, and military maps and routes.

- Books and online databases have military and war records listing soldiers by name, rank, place of birth, death, and ethnicity.

Depending on your ancestry there are more records to explore in other countries. Add any additional information and research to your family tree.

Notes and Clues:

WHAT TO PLACE IN YOUR BINDER(S)

Your binder will be as large or as small as you make it. One day you will pass your binder(s) to your children or someone else in your family. Remember, you are the Ace Genealogy Detective, the keeper of your family's history. Make yourself and your family Proud!!

Favorites
- Baby Picture
- Best Friend
- Family Pictures
- Graduation Pictures
- Relatives
- School Yearbook Pictures
- Teachers

Posters of Your Favorite Things
- Actors/Actresses
- Cars
- Movies
- Sports
- Video Games

Pictures of Your Favorite Treasures
- Awards
- Collector Items
- Hobbies
- Newspaper articles

RESEARCH QUESTIONS

WHAT DID YOU LEARN THE MOST ABOUT YOUR FAMILY?

WHAT DID YOU LEARN THE MOST ABOUT YOUR YOURSELF?

WHAT DID YOUR PARENTS LEARN ABOUT THEIR PARENTS?

DID YOUR PARENTS LEARN ANYTHING NEW ABOUT THEMSELVES?

WHAT SURPRISES DID YOU FIND?

HOW OR WHEN WILL YOU SHARE THIS INFORMATION?

Dedicate your research to the ancestor you learned the most about, or a person you love, to a family member, or to whom you admire.

I Dedicate My Family History To:

_____

(Name)

_____

(Relationship to you)

AND

_____

(Name)

_____

(Relationship to you)

THE END...FOR NOW

ABOUT THE AUTHOR

Ms. Griggs has been the family genealogist for over 35 years. With the help of family, cousins, Internet friends, and others, she has discovered ancestors from various continents and countries. Some countries are Africa, Australia, England, Ireland, and North America.

Denise has researched her maternal ancestors from eighth-century England to southwest Mississippi. She has written a book about it entitled, *A Mulatto Slave, The Events in the Life of Peter Hunt, 1844-1915.* The book received the Phillis Wheatley book award from the Sons and Daughters of the United States Middle Passage and earned a Finalist Award from the Next Generation Indie Book Awards. Ms. Griggs also author's books for children on subjects of diversity and theology.

She is a member of the Daughters of the American Revolution (DAR), formerly serving as Chapter Parliamentarian. She is also a volunteer for the National Park Service, and the Natchez U.S. Colored Troops Monument Committee in Natchez, Mississippi. For the past several years, Denise has been the Exhibit Chair for the board of the Greater Sacramento African American Genealogy Society.

Ms. Griggs graduated with honors from a Christian University. She is presently the Publisher and Owner of Glass Tree Books® and Blue Eclipse Publishing®. She has several family genealogy presentations on her YouTube channel, D.I. Griggs Media.

Denise loves family, friends, history, technology, research, writing, speaking, art, and travel.

OTHER BOOKS BY DENISE I. GRIGGS

Children

Glass Tree Books® https://glasstreebooks.com

<u>Diversity</u> Series featuring Jan and
Denetria *(Includes Worksheets)*:
- The Great Mysterious Adventure
- Our Skin Color Is Our Clothing, Field Trip to the Zoo

<u>Theology</u>
- The Creation Story: Told by the Wise and Majestic Oak Tree
- The Wise Steward Book, for Children Only!

Teens & Young Adults

Blue Eclipse Publishing ® https://blue-eclipse-publishing.com

<u>Genealogy</u>
- A Mulatto Slave, the Events in the Life of Peter Hunt, 1844-1915. *(Includes Topics for Research, Discussion, Worksheets, Historical Timeline, & Family Pictures)*

<u>Theology</u>
- Return to the Table, Beware the Presence, A Christian Thriller

References

- The American Heritage Dictionary of the English Language, New College Edition, William Morris, Editor, Houghton Mifflin Company, Boston, 1969
- The New Merriam-Webster Dictionary, Frederick C. Mish, Editor-in-Chief, Merriam-Webster Inc., Publisher, Springfield, Massachusetts 1989
- https:/www.archives.gov/research/census/online-resources
- https:/www.archives.gov/research/census/soundex
- https://en/wikipedia.org/wiki/Pangaea
- https://aad.archives.gov/aad/
- https://en/wikipedia.org/wiki/Middle_Passage
- https://en/wikipedia.org/wiki/Westward_Expansion_Trails
- Alabama, Arkansas, Louisiana, Mississippi, Oklahoma, Texas, Historic Roads, Paths, Trails, Migration Routes (rootsweb.com)
- https://www.familytreedna.com
- https://www.23andme.com
- https://www.healthonline.com/health/do-identical-twins-have-the-same-dna

Made in the USA
Middletown, DE
26 April 2024

53480491R00031